THE OXFORD SHAKESPEARE

General Editor · Stanley Wells

The Oxford Shakespeare offers new and authoritative editions of Shakespeare's plays in which the early printings have been scrupulously re-examined and interpreted. An introductory essay provides all relevant background information together with an appraisal of critical views and of the play's effects in performance. The detailed commentaries pay particular attention to language and staging. Reprints of sources, music for songs, genealogical tables, maps, etc. are included where necessary; many of the volumes are illustrated, and all contain an index.

JAY L. HALIO, the editor of *The Merchant of Venice* in the Oxford Shakespeare, is Professor of English at the University of Delaware.

THE OXFORD SHAKESPEARE

Currently available in paperback

The rest of the plays are forthcoming.

OXFORD WORLD'S CLASSICS

WILLIAM SHAKESPEARE

The Merchant of Venice

Edited by
JAY L. HALIO

OXFORD
UNIVERSITY PRESS

OXFORD
UNIVERSITY PRESS

Great Clarendon Street, Oxford OX2 6DP

Oxford University Press is a department of the University of Oxford.
It furthers the University's objective of excellence in research, scholarship,
and education by publishing worldwide in

Oxford New York

Athens Auckland Bangkok Bogotá Buenos Aires Cape Town
Chennai Dar es Salaam Delhi Florence Hong Kong Istanbul Karachi
Kolkata Kuala Lumpur Madrid Melbourne Mexico City Mumbai Nairobi
Paris São Paulo Shanghai Singapore Taipei Tokyo Toronto Warsaw

with associated companies in Berlin Ibadan

Oxford is a registered trade mark of Oxford University Press
in the UK and in certain other countries

Published in the United States
by Oxford University Press Inc., New York

© Jay L. Halio 1993

The moral rights of the author have been asserted

Database right Oxford University Press (maker)

First published by the Clarendon Press 1993
First published as a World's Classics paperback 1994
Reissued as an Oxford World's Classics paperback 1998

British Library Cataloguing in Publication Data

Data available

Library of Congress Cataloging in Publication Data

Data available

ISBN 0-19-812925-4 (hbk.)
ISBN 0-19-283424-X (pbk.)

6

Printed in Great Britain by
Clays Ltd, St Ives plc

Dedicated to the memory of my parents

ANNA HALIO (1905–40)

SAMUEL HALIO (1904–91)

PREFACE

I AM deeply grateful to many who have assisted in the work of this edition, especially Thomas Clayton, who read all of the Introduction, to the General Editor, Stanley Wells, who made many useful suggestions and corrections, and to Edwin F. Pritchard, who was a most careful copy-editor. Had it not been for their painstaking labour on my behalf, many more errors and faults would have escaped my notice; those that remain are entirely my responsibility. George Walton Williams and Richard Kennedy not only kindly sent me unpublished manuscripts that illuminated aspects of the text, but also read an earlier version of the textual analysis. James Shapiro made several valuable comments on 'Shakespeare and Semitism'. Meghan Cronin and Christine Volonte, graduate assistants in English at the University of Delaware, helped in the research and checking the typescript. Marcia Halio also read the Introduction in manuscript, and Frances Whistler assisted greatly with the proof-reading. Finally, I owe a large debt of thanks to the personnel and resources of the Morris Library of the University of Delaware and to those of the Folger Shakespeare Library and the Shakespeare Centre Library, Stratford-upon-Avon, for helping to bring this edition to completion.

Note: As this edition was being printed, John Gross's valuable study, *Shylock: Four Hundred Years in the Life of a Legend*, appeared. Unfortunately, I was unable to make use of its many cogent arguments or information, either in the Introduction or the Commentary. Gross is especially useful in some aspects of the stage history, since he surveys a great many more productions than space permits here. He is also extremely interesting in tracing *The Merchant*'s role, and specifically Shylock's, in the history of anti-Semitism in the western world, a major focus of his book, as its subtitle indicates. In his analysis of the background to the play, or to Semitism in England before and during the time of Shakespeare, he covers much the same ground as I do in the first part of this Introduction, but he does not add anything substantially new or different. For that, I suspect we must await the further researches of James Shapiro and others who are investigating the attitudes and actions towards Jews in England and on the Continent during the Middle Ages and the Renaissance. Meanwhile, we have Gross's survey not only of the stage history, but also of the critical commentary down through the centuries, including an illuminating chapter on the responses and reactions to the play by Jewish writers, such as Heinrich Heine, Italo Svevo, Marcel Proust, and Ludwig Lewisohn.

CONTENTS

LIST OF ILLUSTRATIONS